KNOW YOUR SCIENCE TOOLS

LET'S USE MEASURING CUPS

DENNIS LIU

PowerKiDS press

Published in 2027 by The Rosen Publishing Group, Inc.
2544 Clinton Street, Buffalo, NY 14224

First Edition

Editor: Noah Riccardi
Book Design: Claire Vanden Branden

Photo Credits: Cover, p. 1 Africa Studio/Shutterstock.com; p. 5 Crystal Madsen/Shutterstock.com; p. 7 PeopleImages/Shutterstock.com; p. 9 Yes And Yes/Shutterstock.com; p. 11 New Africa/Shutterstock.com; p. 13 Ioana Davies (Drutu)/Shutterstock.com; p. 15 mutsu7211/Shutterstock.com; p. 17 Angellodeco/Shutterstock.com; p. 19 Vladimka Production/Shutterstock.com; p. 21 wavebreakmedia/Shutterstock.com.

Cataloging-in-Publication Data
Names: Liu, Dennis.
Title: Let's use measuring cups / Dennis Liu.
Description: Buffalo, New York : PowerKids Press, 2027. | Series: Know your science tools | Includes glossary and index.
Identifiers: ISBN 9781499459692 (pbk.) | ISBN 9781499459708 (library bound) | ISBN 9781499459715 (ebook)
Subjects: LCSH: Measuring instruments--Juvenile literature. | Units of measurement--Juvenile literature.
Classification: LCC QC100.5 L58 2027 | DDC 681.2--dc23

Manufactured in China

CPSIA Compliance Information: Batch #QS27PK. For Further Information contact Rosen Publishing, at 1-800-237-9932.

CONTENTS

Kitchen and Beyond

Have you helped in the kitchen? If yes, you've probably used a measuring cup. Maybe you needed a half cup of sugar for a cake **recipe**. Adding the exact amount will make the cake taste just right. Measuring is important in both baking and science!

In science, doing **experiments** helps answer questions. Just like recipes, experiments often need exact amounts of solids and liquids. If the amounts aren't right, the experiment won't work. Scientists use special **containers** to hold and measure liquids.

Volume Explained

Volume is the amount of space that matter takes up. Containers with measurements marked on them help us measure the volume of liquids. Some use **units** called cups and ounces. Others use **metric** units called liters and milliliters.

Liquid
600cc/ml

Different Containers

Scientists use different containers as tools to measure volume. Containers called beakers are used to measure and mix liquids. Beakers are shaped like a wide tube. They have a flat bottom. Glass beakers can hold hot liquids.

100

Graduated cylinders are a very common measuring tool. They're very **accurate**. "Graduated" means they're marked with measurement lines. Liquids in these containers are usually measured in milliliters. You might use graduated cylinders in your science class.

A Side View

To see how much liquid is in a graduated cylinder, we have to look at it a certain way. The liquid's surface across the container isn't a straight line—it's curved. That's because the liquid "sticks" to the container's walls!

MADE IN JAPAN
100 ml
TC 20°C
90

First, place the cylinder on a table. Look at the liquid's curve at eye level. The middle of the liquid's surface is lower than the sides. Use the lowest point of the curve as your measurement for the liquid's volume.

50
ml

Other Tools in the Lab

There are more tools scientists use to handle liquids. **Funnels** help them pour liquids without spilling. They use **pipettes** to move small amounts of liquid around. Test tubes store liquids. Scientists may wear special glasses to guard their eyes from harmful or hot liquids.

Lab Safety

If your school has a lab, you might use measuring cups in experiments. When you're in the lab mixing liquids, be safe. Only mix liquids your teacher tells you to mix. Be sure to wear safety glasses, too. Safe science is fun science!

GLOSSARY

accurate: Free from mistakes, or exact.

containers: Objects that can hold something.

experiments: Scientific tests done to figure something out.

funnels: Tools shaped like a hollow cone with a tube reaching down from the point.

metric: Part of a system of measurements based on units such as the liter and meter.

pipettes: Tools that use suction to hold liquids.

recipe: A set of instructions for making food.

units: Amounts of length, weight, volume, or other measurements.

FOR MORE INFORMATION

BOOKS

Lake, Theia. *Measuring in the Kitchen*. Buffalo, NY: Rosen Publishing, 2024.

O'Daly, Anne. *Measuring Volume*. Buffalo, NY: Rosen Publishing, 2024.

WEBSITES

Britannica Kids: Measurement
kids.britannica.com/kids/article/measurement/399538
Learn about measuring cups and other ways to measure.

PBS LearningMedia: Understanding Concepts of Volume and Measurement
thinktv.pbslearningmedia.org/resource/mwnet-math-md-babyblu/understanding-concepts-of-volume-and-measurement-biancas-babysitting-blues/
See measurements of volume in action.

Publisher's note to educators and parents: Our editors have carefully reviewed these websites to ensure that they are suitable for students. Many websites change frequently, however, and we cannot guarantee that a site's future contents will continue to meet our high standards of quality and educational value. Be advised that students should be closely supervised whenever they access the internet.

INDEX